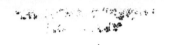

Facts About

The Far Planets

DONNA BAILEY

STECK-VAUGHN
LIBRARY
A Division of Steck-Vaughn Company
Austin, Texas

How to Use This Book

This book tells you many things about the planets farthest from the Sun. There is a Table of Contents on the next page. It shows you what each double page of the book is about. For example, pages 10 and 11 tell you about "Jupiter: the Giant."

On many of these pages you will find words that are printed in **bold** type. The bold type shows you that these words are in the Glossary on pages 46 and 47. The Glossary explains the meaning of some words that may be new to you.

At the very end of the book there is an Index. The Index tells you where to find certain words in the book. For example, you can use it to look up words like space probes, Solar System, orbit, and many other words to do with the far planets.

© Copyright 1991, text, Steck-Vaughn Company

Library of Congress Cataloging-in-Publication Data

Bailey, Donna.
  The far planets / written by Donna Bailey.
    p.   cm.—(Facts about)
  Includes index.
  Summary: Examines the five known planets that lie outside the orbit of Mars, discussing their history, composition, moons, and possible planetary neighbors beyond Pluto.
  ISBN 0-8114-2524-X
  1. Outer planets—Juvenile literature. [1. Outer planets. 2. Planets.] I. Title. II. Series: Facts about (Austin, Tex.)
QB639.B35 1991   90-40081
523.4—dc20   CIP AC

Printed and bound in the United States of America
  2 3 4 5 6 7 8 9 0 LB 95 94 93 92

Contents

Introduction

The world we live on is a **planet** called Earth. The Earth is one of nine planets that travel around the **Sun**.

The planets Jupiter, Saturn, Uranus, Neptune, and Pluto are the farthest from the Sun so they are called the outer planets.

Mercury, Venus, Earth, and Mars are the inner planets, or those that are nearest the Sun.

The Solar System

Sun

Jupiter

Mercury

Venus

Earth

Mars

inner planets

The Sun, the nine planets, and their **moons** make up the **Solar System**.

The Solar System is huge. Pluto is the most distant planet from the Sun. Pluto is nearly 50 times farther away from the Sun than our Earth. Pluto moves in an **orbit** as far as 4,582 billion miles away from the Sun. It is very cold and dark where Pluto is.

The photograph shows the storm clouds that surround the planet Jupiter. The surface of Jupiter is covered with a hot liquid. Nothing could live there.

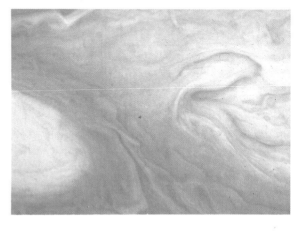

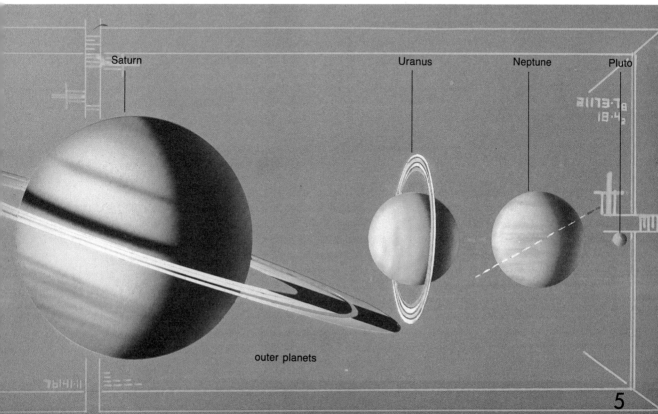

outer planets

Planets in History

Long ago people thought that gods and goddesses lived on the planets. They named the planets after them and built temples in their honor. The photo shows the ruins of the temple of Saturn in Rome.

Scientists use **telescopes** to study the planets and stars. A Dutch **astronomer**, Hans Lippershey, built the first telescope in 1608. Astronomers then discovered that the planets are round worlds like our Earth. They could see the rings around Saturn, and moons in orbit around Jupiter. In 1781 William Hershel, an Englishman, found the planet Uranus.

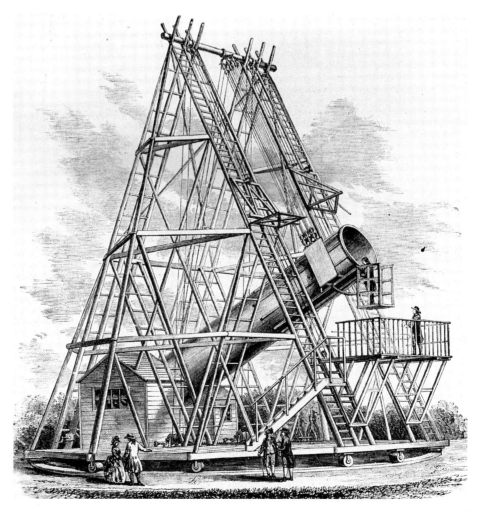

William Hershel's telescope

Exploring Space

Space probes have taken photographs of most of the planets and their moons. Pioneer 10 was the first space probe to fly past one of the outer planets. It flew past Jupiter in 1973. A year later Pioneer 11 flew past Jupiter and Saturn. Voyager 2 flew past Uranus in 1986.

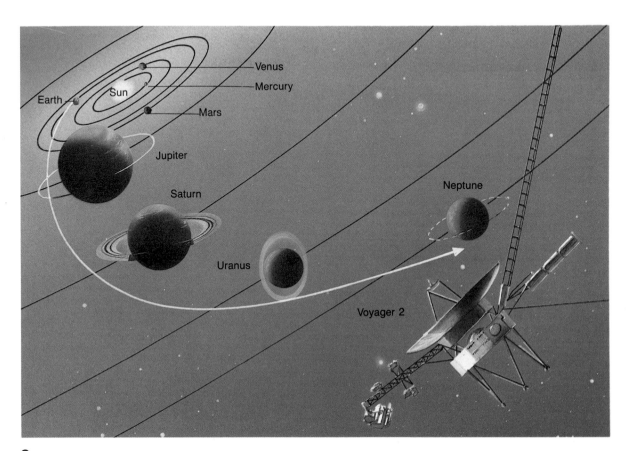

Venus

Mercury

Earth

Sun

Mars

Jupiter

Saturn

Uranus

Neptune

Voyager 2

Pioneer 10 is prepared for its journey into space

Voyager 2 is still moving through space. In 1989 it became the first space probe to fly past the planet Neptune. Space probes have now visited all the planets except Pluto, which is the farthest away.

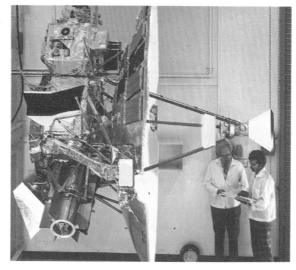

Voyager 1 flying past the planet Saturn

Space probes take close-up photographs as they fly past the planets. **Radio signals** send these photographs back to Earth.

9

Jupiter: The Giant

Jupiter is the biggest planet of all. It is 11 times wider than Earth, and five times farther away from the Sun. Jupiter is the nearest outer planet to Earth. We can see it easily at night because it shines with a yellow light.

If you look at Jupiter through a telescope you can see that the planet looks like a round disk with a pattern of markings on it. You can see these markings quite clearly in our close-up view sent back to Earth by the space probe Voyager I.

Facts about Jupiter

Diameter	88,000 miles
Mass	318 times that of Earth
Distance from the Sun	480 million miles
Period of rotation	9 hours, 50 minutes
Period of revolution	11.9 years
Tilt of axis	3°
Gravity on the surface	2.7 times that of Earth
Average temperature	-240°F
Atmosphere	hydrogen, helium
Number of moons	16

Earth   Jupiter

Jupiter: Inside the Planet

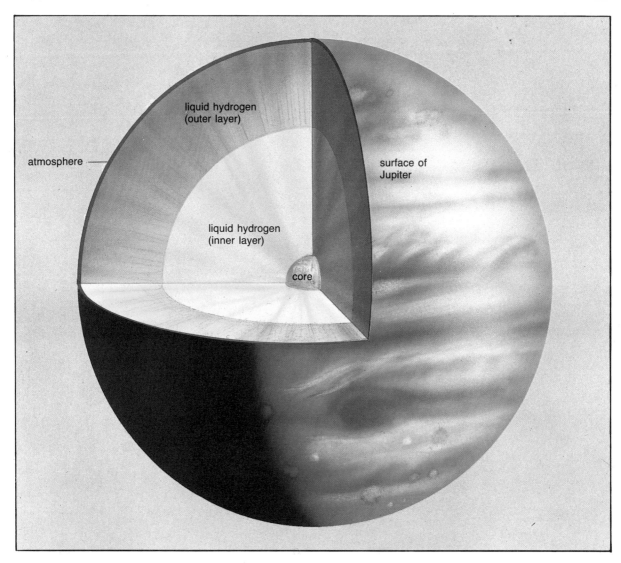

atmosphere

liquid hydrogen
(outer layer)

liquid hydrogen
(inner layer)

core

surface of
Jupiter

Jupiter is not a solid planet made of rocks.
It is made up mostly of liquid **hydrogen**.
At the center of the planet Jupiter is
a small rocky **core**.

Photographs show that huge bands of storm clouds circle the whole planet.

Jupiter gets very little heat from the Sun because it is so far away. The planet makes its own heat deep inside its core. The heat spreads evenly over the whole planet and rises up through the layers of liquid hydrogen to the surface.

The picture shows how the hot gas then rises into the **atmosphere**. Finally the hot gas moves into the belts of cooler gases surrounding the planet.

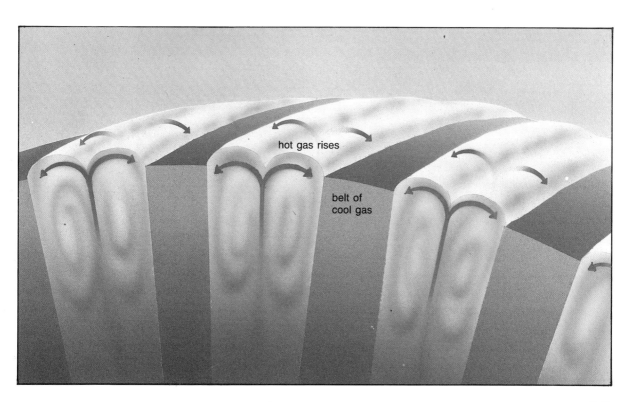

hot gas rises

belt of cool gas

Jupiter: The Storm Clouds

Jupiter is a very colorful sight in the Solar System. Bands of bright colors surround the whole planet. These are made by storm clouds carried by winds which howl around Jupiter at speeds of 300 miles an hour. Lightning flashes through these clouds of gas.

Rays from the Sun strike the clouds as well, making other gases. One of these gases is **ammonia** and another is the gas **hydrogen sulfide.** These gases mix together to make frozen **crystals** of gas and drops of water. The atmosphere of Jupiter is very cold at the top and very hot at the bottom.

14

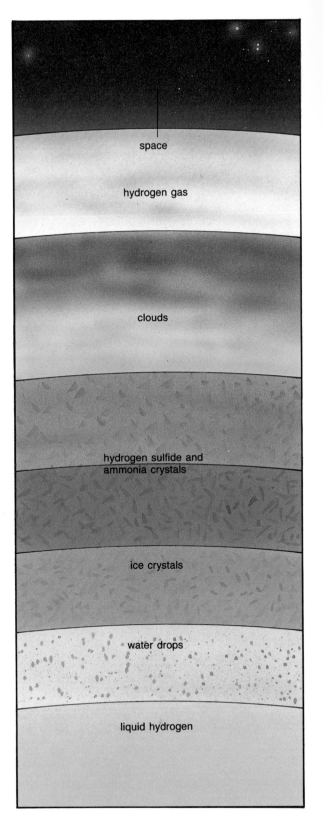

space

hydrogen gas

clouds

hydrogen sulfide and
ammonia crystals

ice crystals

water drops

liquid hydrogen

The biggest shape we can see on Jupiter
is a bright red oval called the Great
Red Spot. This is made by swirling
clouds that whirl around, like **hurricanes**
on Earth. These swirling gases have
been spinning around like this for a
very long time.

Jupiter: Close Neighbors

Jupiter's moons

Name	Diameter (mi.)	Distance from Jupiter (mi.)
Metis	25	80,000
Adrastea	15	80,150
Amalthea	130	113,000
Thebe	62	138,000
Io	2,256	262,000
Europa	1,950	417,000
Ganymede	3,270	665,000
Callisto	2,983	1,168,000
Leda	6	6,894,000
Himalia	112	7,134,000
Lysithea	15	7,283,000
Elara	50	7,293,000
Ananke	15	13,170,000
Carme	19	14,000,000
Pasiphaë	25	14,600,000
Sinope	19	14,725,000

Jupiter has 16 moons that travel around it, just as our Moon orbits the Earth. The Voyager space probes found that Jupiter has a thin **ring** around it. The photograph shows the ring is a thin orange band made of specks of dust. You cannot see the ring through a telescope because it is very faint.

The four moons nearest to Jupiter are all very small. Then come four big moons. The inner two of these large moons are called Io and Europa.

Europa is very smooth and is covered with ice. The photograph (above), taken by a Voyager probe, shows that the ice is cracked and so Europa is covered in lines.

Io is covered by **volcanoes** that spurt out hot, liquid, and yellow **sulfur**.

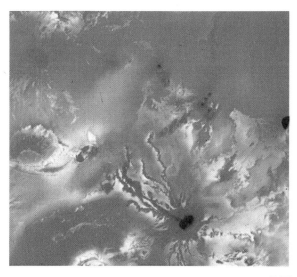

Jupiter: The Outer Moons

The outer two of Jupiter's big moons
are called Ganymede and Callisto.

The surfaces of both Ganymede and
Callisto are made of ice and rock.
A lot of the ice is dirty because it is
mixed with very old rocks.

Parts of Ganymede are covered with
strange patterns of lines. Movements
of the ice and rock have made these long
cracks in the surface.

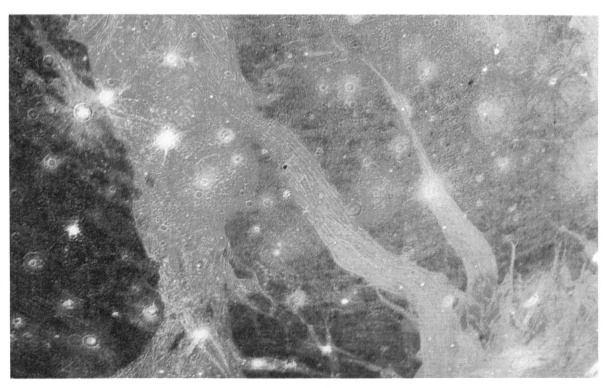

Callisto has a huge area of rings of
ridges which astronomers call Valhalla.
Valhalla was formed when a big
meteorite crashed into the moon and
melted some of the ice. This made
big ripples that later froze solid
to make the ridges.

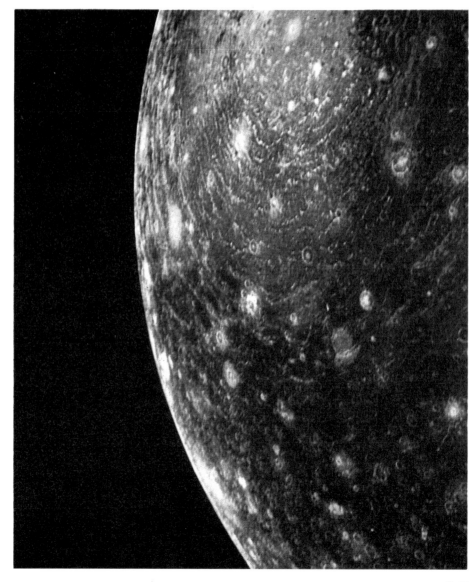

**the rings of
Valhalla on
the moon
Callisto**

Jupiter: The Galileo Probe

The Galileo space probe has lots of new scientific equipment inside it. It was launched in 1989.

Galileo will fly past Jupiter and its moons in 1995. It will take six years to reach Jupiter. On the way, it is likely to fly past an **asteroid** and send back photographs.

Galileo is in two parts. About 150 days before the probe reaches Jupiter, it will split in two. One part of it will head straight for Jupiter. It will float down to the planet by parachute, taking scientific measurements. The other section will go into orbit around Jupiter.

21

Saturn: Planet of Beauty

Saturn looks like a bright **star** in the night sky. It is surrounded by wide rings and over 20 moons. It is the most beautiful planet in the Solar System.

Saturn is a very large planet. It is like Jupiter except for its wide rings. Like Jupiter, Saturn is covered by an ocean of hot liquid hydrogen. It has a core of rock that is the same size as Earth.

Storm clouds circle the planet and strong winds blow at 1,120 miles an hour. There are large spots in the clouds around Saturn. The spots are smaller than Jupiter's Great Red Spot.

In 1612 Galileo made these drawings of Saturn. They look like three planets close together.

Facts about Saturn	
Diameter	71,000 miles
Mass	95 times that of Earth
Distance from the Sun	900 million miles
Period of rotation	10 hours, 40 minutes
Period of revolution	29.5 years
Tilt of axis	27°
Gravity on the surface	1.2 times that of Earth
Temperature	-300°F
Atmosphere	hydrogen, helium
Number of moons	possibly 23

Earth   Saturn

The Voyager space probe took photographs of Saturn and its rings. These showed up the light and dark bands which are the gases of the planet's atmosphere.

Saturn and its rings

Saturn: The Rings

When we look through a telescope at Saturn, we can see three broad rings. The rings are made of bits of ice which move in circles around the planet. The outer ring or A ring is next to a dark gap, the Cassini Division. The central ring is the B ring and the inner ring or C ring, is much fainter than the other two.

Photographs from Pioneer and Voyager showed that Saturn has four other rings. Most of these rings are very faint. Voyager found that all the rings are only 15 to 100 feet deep. But the rings are 370,000 miles across.

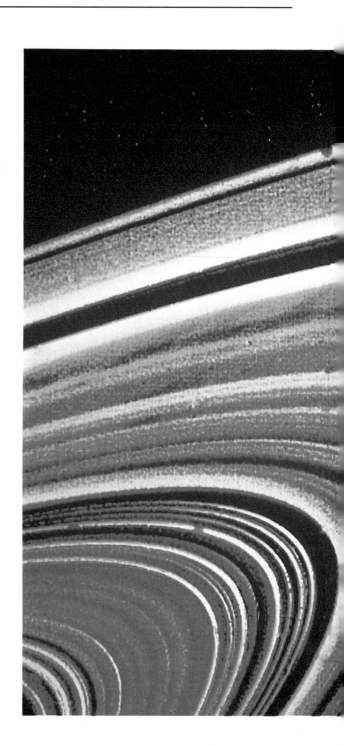

Astronomers are not sure why the rings
of Saturn have different colors.
Perhaps the ice in the rings is not
clean, but full of rocks and dust.

Saturn: The Inner Moons

Astronomers think Saturn could have as many as 23 moons, but little is known about some of them.
Some of them are very wide.

Dione, one of Saturn's icy inner moons, is covered with **craters**.

Saturn's Inner Moons		
Name	Diameter (miles)	Distance from Saturn (miles)
Atlas	19	86,063
Inner Shepherd	63	87,094
Outer Shepherd	50	88,562
Janus	119	94,638
Epimetheus	75	94,669
Mimas	244	115,938
Enceladus	313	148,750
Tethys	663	184,188
Telesto	16	184,188
Calypso	16	184,188
Dione	700	235,875
Dione B	19	235,875
Rhea	956	329,375

Dione is one-third the size of Earth's moon

Voyager 2 took this photograph of
Enceladus, another of Saturn's inner
moons. Enceladus is made of ice and rock,
and is covered with craters and ridges.
It's one-sixth the size of Earth's moon.

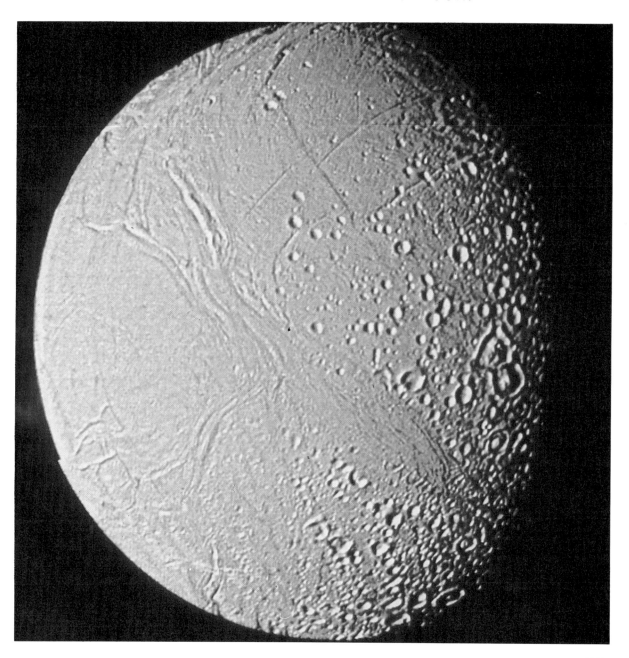

Saturn: The Outer Moons

Titan, the first of the outer moons of Saturn, is the second largest moon in the Solar System. The photo shows that Titan is surrounded by an orange fog made from a mixture of **nitrogen** and **methane**.

The surface of Titan is very cold. Inside it is made of ice with a core of rock.

Scientists think Titan's surface may be covered by liquid methane or brown snow made from methane. Long ago Earth might have been like Titan is now.

Facts about Titan	
Diameter	3,200 miles
Distance from Saturn	760,000 miles
Surface temperature	-300°F
Pressure of atmosphere	1.6 times Earth
Period of rotation and revolution	15.9 days
Gravity on the surface	1/6 that of Earth

Beyond Titan there are three more moons. The photo shows Iapetus, which is covered in light and dark rocks. It is marked by craters. Iapetus is less than a quarter of the size of Titan.

Saturn's outermost moon, Phoebe, goes around Saturn the opposite way to all the other moons.

Saturn's Outer Moons		
Name	Diameter (miles)	Distance from Saturn (miles)
Hyperion	155	920,000
Iapetus	907	2,213,000
Phoebe	137	8,050,000

Uranus: The Tilted Planet

Uranus is so faint that you can barely
see it without a telescope.
It is the third largest planet in the
Solar System, and it has five moons.
Voyager 2 flew past Uranus in 1986 and
sent back very clear photographs of
the planet, its rings, and its moons.
The photographs show that the whole
planet is covered by a blue-green fog.
The atmosphere contains the gases
hydrogen, **helium**, and methane.
Scientists think the surface of Uranus
is covered with an ocean of hot water.

Facts about Uranus	
Diameter	32,000 miles
Mass	15 times that of Earth
Distance from the Sun	1.8 billion miles
Period of rotation	17 hours, 15 minutes
Period of revolution	84 years
Tilt of axis	98°
Gravity on the surface	9/10 of that on Earth
Temperature	-350°F
Atmosphere	hydrogen, helium, methane
Moons	15

Earth   Uranus

Scientists have found out a very strange fact about Uranus. The planet is lying on its side. The reason for this big tilt may be that Uranus was once hit by an asteroid which turned the planet over.

2029

S

N

2008

S

N

Earth

Sun

S

N

1966

orbit of
Uranus

S

N

1987

Uranus: Rings and Moons

The picture shows Uranus and its rings as seen from its moon, Miranda.

Miranda is the nearest moon to Uranus

This picture shows the dark chunks of
ice that make the rings around Uranus.
Voyager 2 found ten of these rings as it
flew past the planet.

Voyager also spotted ten small moons
in orbit around Uranus, between the rings
and Miranda. The moons of Uranus have
huge white and dark patches that
scientists think are made of ice mixed
with frozen gases.

The larger moons of Uranus

Name	Diameter (miles)	Distance from Uranus (miles)
Miranda	310	81,000
Ariel	800	119,000
Umbriel	680	166,000
Titania	995	272,000
Oberon	995	364,000

Titania   Oberon   Ariel

Umbriel   Miranda

Neptune: The Blue Planet

Neptune is almost as large as Uranus. It is the fourth biggest planet in the Solar System. It is so far away from Earth that it looks very faint in the night sky.

When Voyager 2 flew past Neptune on August 25, 1989, it sent back photographs of the planet, showing that its bright blue surface is covered with light and dark clouds.

Like Uranus, the surface of Neptune is covered with water. The clouds are made from methane gas that has frozen. There may also be high winds on Neptune.

Facts about Neptune

Diameter	31,000 miles
Mass	17 times that of Earth
Distance from the Sun	2.8 billion miles
Period of rotation	18 hours
Period of revolution	165 years
Tilt of axis	29°
Gravity on the surface	1.1 times that of Earth
Temperature	-360°F
Atmosphere	hydrogen, helium, methane
Moons	2

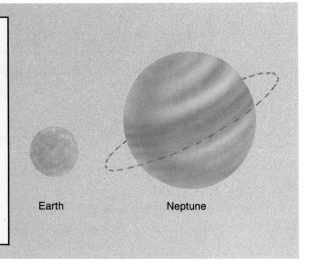

Earth   Neptune

Voyager 2 flew past Neptune and took photographs

35

Neptune: Two Moons

Neptune has two moons which circle it. One is a tiny world called Nereid.

Neptune's other moon, Triton, is the fourth largest moon that we know of. Triton goes around Neptune in the opposite direction of most other moons. Scientists think Triton may have an atmosphere of methane and nitrogen.

Pluto: The Ninth Planet

Most of the time Pluto is the farthest planet from the Sun. During part of its orbit Pluto comes nearer to the Sun than Neptune. It was in this part of its orbit in 1990. In 1999 it will become the most distant planet again.

Pluto is smaller than any other planet. It is even smaller than our Moon. Most of its atmosphere consists of methane gas.

Pluto has a tiny moon of its own called Charon, which is about half the size of Pluto.

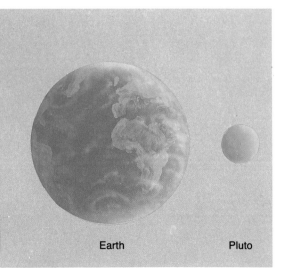

Facts about Pluto

Diameter	1,367 miles
Mass	1/450 that of Earth
Distance from the Sun	3.6 billion miles
Period of rotation	6 days, 9 hours, 18 minutes
Period of revolution	248 years
Tilt of axis	118°
Gravity on the surface	1/13 that of Earth
Temperature	-360°F
Atmosphere	unknown
Moons	1

Earth   Pluto

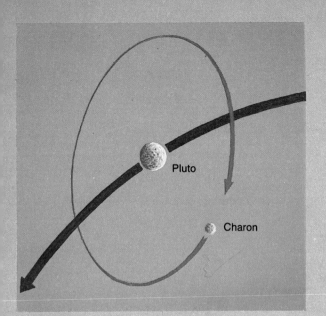

Sun

Pluto

Charon

**Charon circles in orbit
around Pluto**

Pluto

**a spacecraft from Earth
would take at least ten
years to reach Pluto**

Planet X?

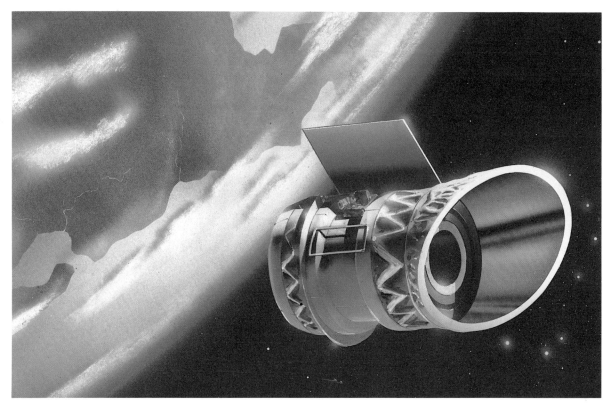

Some scientists think there is another
planet that has not yet been discovered.
This picture shows IRAS, an **Infra-Red
Astronomy Satellite**, which looks for
heat rays coming from space.
Planets make their own heat as well as
reflecting heat from the Sun.
Scientists hope that IRAS will help
them find Planet X.

If Planet X does exist, it should be in a distant orbit far beyond Pluto.

The photograph shows the Goldstone Tracking Station in California which tracks probes traveling beyond Jupiter. Astronomers hope that the Pioneer and Voyager space probes will send back signals from space that would tell us where the missing planet is.

Comets in Space

A comet is a ball of dust and ice that orbits the Sun. Some of the ice boils near the Sun and streams out to make a long "tail" of dust and gas.

The comet does not usually fall into the Sun. It swings around the Sun then heads back into space. It never returns.

As a comet flies away from the Sun it cools down. The tail shrinks and disappears. The comet leaves a trail of dust behind. Bits of dust entering Earth's atmosphere become **shooting stars**.

a comet glows in the night sky

Halley and Beyond

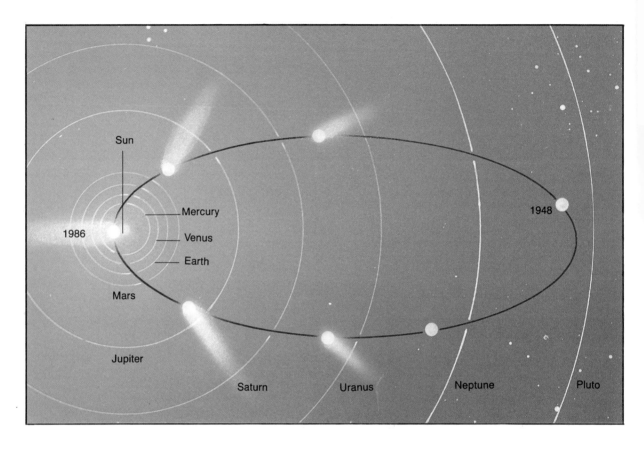

Halley's comet is the most famous comet.
Its orbit led it past the Earth in 1986.
It comes back every 76 years, so it
will not be seen again until the year 2061.

When Halley's comet came near the
Earth in 1986, the space probe Giotto
was sent to look at it. Giotto flew
right into the comet's tail.

the Giotto probe on its way to Halley's comet

Giotto came within 373 miles of
the center of the comet. The probe
sent back pictures of the center
of the comet, which showed it was about
10 miles long and covered with a
black dust or tar.

Glossary

ammonia a gas that has a very strong smell and no color.

asteroid a tiny planet made out of rock that orbits the Sun.

astronomer someone who studies the stars, planets, and other objects in space.

atmosphere the layer of gases that surround a planet or a star.

core the center of something.

crater a bowl-shaped hollow. The surfaces of some planets and moons are covered with craters.

crystals solid pieces of matter with different shapes and surfaces.

helium a gas that is the second lightest in the Universe. Hydrogen is the lightest gas.

hurricanes very strong winds. On Earth, hurricanes can blow at speeds of more than 80 miles an hour.

hydrogen the lightest gas in the Universe.

hydrogen sulfide a colorless gas that smells like rotten eggs.

Infra-Red Astronomy Satellite a type of satellite that looks for heat rays coming from space. A satellite is a spacecraft that orbits the Earth.

meteorite a piece of rock or metal from space that can pass through a planet's atmosphere without burning up. It crashes onto the surface of the planet.

methane a colorless gas that can burn. It is found underground on Earth and is present in many planets.

moon a smaller body that travels around a planet. The planet Jupiter has 16 moons. The planet Earth has only one moon.

nitrogen a gas found in the atmosphere of some planets. It has no color, taste, or smell. It does not burn.

orbit a path through space made by one thing going around another. The Earth moves in orbit around the Sun.

planet a body in space that moves around a star like the Sun. The planet shines by reflecting the light of the star.

radio signals messages sent by using invisible waves that travel through air or space.

ring a band of rock, ice, dust or frozen gas circling a planet.

shooting star a streak of light seen when a meteor or dust enters the Earth's atmosphere and burns up.

Solar System the Sun and all the objects that orbit it, such as their planets and their moons.

space probe a machine sent from Earth to study objects in space. It does not have people on board.

star a glowing ball of gas that gives off its own light and heat. The Sun is a star.

sulfur a yellow, solid substance that is found in the Earth and other bodies in the Solar System. It burns with a blue flame.

Sun our home star, from which we receive all our heat and light.

telescope an instrument for looking at distant objects, or for picking up rays that come from them.

volcano a type of mountain that is formed when very hot liquid rock is forced up from deep inside a planet. The liquid cools leaving a mountain of rock.

Photographic credits (t=top b=bottom l=left r=right)
cover: NASA/Science photo Library; title page NASA/Science Photo Library
5 Science Photo Library; 6 ZEFA; 7 Ann Ronan Picture Library; 9t, 9b Science Photo Library; 11 NASA; 15, 16, 17t, 17b, 18, 19, 20/21 Science Photo Library; 22 Ann Ronan Picture Library; 23, 24/25, 26, 27, 28, 29, 30, 33, 35, 41, 42, 43, 45 Science Photo Library

Index

© Heinemann Children's Reference 1990
Artwork © BLA Publishing Limited 1987

Material used in this book first appeared in
Macmillan World Library: *The Outer Planets*.
Published by Heinemann Children's
Reference.